W9-CRD-493

AKASHIC RECORDS

AKASHIC RECORDS

PAST LIVES & NEW DIRECTIONS

ROBERT CHANEY

Published by

Astara

792 W. Arrow Highway
Upland, CA 91786

Books by the Author

The Power of Your Own Medicine
Ten Steps to Self Fulfillment
The Inner Way
Mysticism—The Journey Within
The Essenes and Their Ancient Mysteries
Unfolding the Third Eye
Think on New Levels
The Jeweled Tree of Life
Occult Hypnotism
Reincarnation: Cycle of Opportunity
Transmutation: How the Alchemists
Turned Lead into Gold

Cover By:
Steve Doolittle

Library of Congress
Catalogue Card
#95-83812

ISBN #0-918936-31-4

Printed in the United States of America

Contents

Acknowledgements

A writer often feels like a drowning person. At least I frequently do. Those who threw lifelines to me, and pulled me through the flood, include my wife and daughter, Earlyne and Sita Chaney, and professional associates Pam Rau, Steve Doolittle, Beth Hickerson and Jeffrey Meyer. Each deserves credit for being an important part of this book.

Dedication

This book is dedicated to two legendary persons—one a renowned scientist, the other a famed mystic. One afternoon they met for an hour to discuss their respective views.

A group of followers of each waited outside the meeting place, expecting a lively debate and certain their champion would be victorious. They surged forward as the two emerged.

The scientist spoke to his advocates, saying, "Everything that he sees, I know."

The mystic then spoke to his followers, saying, "Everything that he knows, I see."

And everyone was happy!

Preface

Dear Reader—

Unless it has happened on another planet, no one I know of has written a book about the Akashic Records. The problem is that you can't see, hear, smell, taste or touch them with your physical senses.

But there are some five-dimensional seekers who aren't inhibited by dimensional limitations. You may be among them. If so, you seek for what is beyond whatever is beyond matter, and even beyond that. And more importantly, as such a one you probably want to know what the Akashic Records mean to you. How can they help you. Why should you know about them. Do they contribute to your strength, growth, health, spiritual evolvement.

Note, please, that I haven't placed question marks after those questions. That's because I don't think of them as questions but as indicators of what you have a right to know about one of the great cosmic mysteries—the Akashic Records.

This age-old mystery is one we can truly begin to appreciate only by the light of modern science. The mystery is the Akashic Records, the eternal record of individual lives, the Book of God's Remembrance. The modern science is the computer.

Is comparing a spiritual concept, such as the Akashic Records, with an inanimate device such as a computer, a strange way to approach this subject? Certainly not more so than was the book *Zen, and the Art of Motorcycle Maintenance*, which is still a popular title. Or the book *The Tao of Physics*, equally popular and pertinent to one's spiritual evolvement.

Some may suggest to you that the computer is a dehumanizing device. Books have included this thought, yet the publication and distribution of those very books would not have been possible without the computer they malign. The computer isn't the problem. It's the people who use them.

Anything can be misused but that's no reason to discredit it. In recent history the bathtub, telephone, automobile, radio, television and space travel (to name a few) have been the subject of the same attack. Yet they all have contributed to the health and productivity of humankind.

Productivity. Is that the computer's only contribution? Absolutely not. Education, creativity, industry, the health of every person on earth, all are enhanced by the computer. And that list is but a beginning. In home after home the computer is becoming the family's best friend.

But there are other and higher aspects of human life to which the computer as an analogy can be applied to great advantage. Understanding more of the life interaction between this world and the next, spiritual knowledge of age-old mysteries in the life of every human being, and awareness of the life of the soul both in and out of the body—all this and more offers us merely a point of departure on a great adventure.

The spiritual secrets which the computer will help us reveal to ourselves may be the greatest of all its contributions to your life.

The Akashic Records, a spiritual place where a record of your life is kept, have long been the subject of speculation. But we now have the opportunity to understand them, and that is the important mystery we approach in this book. Let us remember that the best of all treasures are those you find in yourself, and for yourself. *Inner discovery*, not the computer, is the reason for this book.

In ways never before possible, the computer age gives us the analogy for understanding, experiencing and benefitting from the Akashic Records. There are a truly surprising number of corollaries between the computer you may be using now, in your home, office, or school, and the way your life events are recorded in a cosmic repository. The Akashic Records and the computer serve the same function: both are extensions of the human individual, one on the level of higher reality and one on this physical level.

If you aren't familiar with computers don't be put off by tne fact that we're going to use them to help us understand the Akashic Records. When it comes to computers I know next to nothing! There was a time when my computer and I weren't friends. It didn't seem to understand me very well, and I didn't understand it at all. But when we grew (or *I* grew) to know each other we came to the point of realizing that we were experiencing a "family" relationship. Everything was much better after that. Then I began to realize that my computer was teaching me the inner spiritual workings of a concept long held but not really understood— the Akashic Records.

I'll use only half a dozen of the simplest computer terms to illustrate just how the Akashic Records are an integral aspect of your total life. I'll attempt to illustrate how you can relate to those Records on a level of reality heretofore considered impossible.

Probably every eight-year-old child is familiar with the computer terms in the following text, and their meaning to the computer user. This information is going to take us on a journey the wisest of ancients would never have believed, a magic carpet ride to the land of understanding one of the great esoteric mysteries of a higher life. So, come along with me now and let's begin our magical journey.

— Robert Chaney

P.S. But remember...this isn't a book about computers. It's about you. And it's about your part in the emerging spiritual science of a new level of reality....

1

FILE...is a computer term for a specific electromagnetic record of information. For our purpose in studying the Akashic Records, it is the vibrational record of all the important events in your life.

Have you ever wondered about the Akashic Records—those nebulous vibrational archives on which your acts and feelings are recorded? And which record the deeds, good or ill, of every human being?

What are these Records? Where are they? Are they permanent or can they be changed? Why do they exist? Do they serve a useful purpose in your life? Can you "read" them for details of a past life...or the reasons for problems in your present life?

Answers to these questions are found in the esoteric traditions of thousands of years ago—and in the experiences of moderns such as yourself. Answers are found through parallels with modern science—and through that type of spiritual speculation which ultimately leads to a realization of reality.

But first, let us examine the word *Akasha*. It has long

existed in the mystical philosophy of India, with the literal meaning of *sky*. However, like words in any language, it has other meanings. It also means *space*, with the further meaning of distinguishing the difference between the sky directly overhead and the space existing throughout our galaxy.

The word *Akasha* possesses a still greater meaning: *Cosmic Sky*—not limited to intergalactic space but also space on a higher vibrational level. In other words, it includes, space in the loftier dimensions of life, the afterworld of every religion, the source from which creation flowed, the domain of the Divine.

An acceptance of this higher dimensional cosmic sky leads us to consideration of an astounding idea, an idea of unlimited scope, possibly too brash for modern science to ponder.

> *Perhaps the vibrational threads of a single life, yours for instance, permeate the entire universe, interacting with other vibrational energies, both here and as distant as your consciousness will accept.*

Just as the words and music of a song are preserved on audio tape, or a CD (compact disk), so is the story of your life saved in the Akashic Records. The stories of your triumphs and tragedies, your mistakes and your corrections of them, your debts and repayments, your sorrows and joys—all are included in the Akashic Records.

If the Akashic Records contain the accumulated life facts of everyone in existence, is there really enough space in the universe to include it all? Of course, and with plenty of space remaining to accommodate thousands of generations in the future. Computer science illustrates this fact for us.

A CD (compact disk), for example, can hold an enormous amount of information. Think for a moment of the size of a football field—300 feet long and 160 feet wide. If you covered a football field with CDs to a height of only three and a half inches, they could contain records of the life events for 250,000,000,000 people. Yes, two hundred and fifty *billion* people! That's roughly fifty times the population of the earth today. Each single disk could hold the records for 16,000 people. So there's enough space in universal primary substance for unnumbered quintillions of records. Staggering! But contributing to the understanding that Akashic Records are indeed a possibility.

How long have you been adding to your File in the Akashic Records? No specific numerical answer to such a question is possible.

According to mystical science: before the world was, human souls were. The precession of solar systems, such as ours, has been occurring for an unknown number of eons. How many times our galaxy has made its journey 'round and 'round we know not, cycles of light and darkness following each other endlessly, around a great magnetic pole or sun. So we've been involved with the recording element of primary substance for a time span too great for the human consciousness to grasp.

Those who are known to us as ancients, dating back beyond the glory days of lofty civilizations in Egypt, China, and India, possibly once possessed and then lost the technology which might have explained the Akashic Records as we can understand them today.

Even in Biblical times there may have been a glimmer of understanding of the vibrational impact caused by human thoughts and acts. Written records of days long past give us fascinating information indicating that people of earlier times accepted something akin to the Akashic Records.

For example, the biblical *Book of Joshua* tells how that prophet turned his followers from the worship of many gods to the acceptance of the One. He asked them to pledge their allegiance to the one God, which they did. He then "took a great stone," showed it to the people and said, "Behold, this stone shall be a witness to us; for *it hath heard all the words* of the Lord which he spake unto us: it shall be therefore a witness unto you, lest ye deny your God."

Can a stone hear? Was Joshua saying that "the words" were of sufficient vibrational intensity to create an influence on the vibrational matter of the stone? Our speculation can only tell us that in the light of modern computer science such a result might be possible. (Personally I like the possibility and think it should be scientifically researched.)

Our speculation concerning the concept of the Akashic Records can be advanced still further by the description of a prophetic statement involving the Archangel Michael, described in the *Book of Daniel*.

The first declaration in the final chapter of the *Book of Daniel* contains a thought which could be interpreted as an offhand reference to the Akashic Records. The prophet is quoted as saying, "And at that time shall Michael stand up...and there shall be a time of trouble...and at that time thy people shall be delivered, *every one that shall be found written in the book*."

Neither the name nor nature of the book is specified. But esotericists have long inferred that it was *The Book of Life*, a vibrational record of the lives of all people. Michael was traditionally the recorder and keeper of this book.

Then a brief scriptural passage in the *Book of Malachi* refers to the Akashic Records in these words: "Then they that feared the Lord spake often one to another: and the Lord harkened and heard it, and *a book of remembrance* was written before him for them...that thought upon his name."

And a short mystical statement in Paul's *Second Epistle to the Corinthians*: "For you are known to be the epistle of Christ ministered by us, written not with ink, but with the Spirit of the living God; *not on tablets of stone, but on tablets of the living heart.*" (Translated from the Aramaic by Dr. George Lamsa.)

Where are the Akashic Records?

Most of the ancient spiritual philosophies, whether in primitive or sophisticated form, posited an original Source from which substance in the form of high vibrational energy flowed throughout an unlimited area of space. This occurred under the direction of "Original Intelligence," in the guise of a wide variety of names and symbols. Such high vibrational energy may be thought of as *primary substance.* And this primary substance permeates all that is. We have no instrument to detect it, let alone measure it.

All that is, on any plane of life, is in primary substance. Translated into Christianity's idiom, it is symbolized by the idea that "I am in the Father, and the Father is in me." We may say, then, that the Akashic Records are the imprint of the Self on the eternal, universal, electromagnetic atmosphere of primary substance. That substance is everywhere. The particular "wavelength" of that substance which is of a high spiritual level, close to the "wavelength" of the original Source, is the one on which the Akashic Records are imprinted. That is where the personal archive of your life is located.

But *where*, we ask, for our normal and limited level of consciousness requires a specific point in space. It is now that, if it hasn't already occurred, you must enlarge the acceptance range of your consciousness to consider an esoteric (or hidden) concept which can be fully understood only on a much higher level of reality than normal.

Can you point to any place in space and say, "There it is!" Are the Records in the Gobi Desert, or Fargo, North Dakota? Or any other visible site?

The Records, in primary substance, are basic to the universal ethers so *they are everywhere*. Wherever you stand, sit or lie down, they are there. On earth, on the moon, on the most distant planet, wherever it may be, they are there.

Your "page," or in computer language "file," may be written on or read from wherever you are. You are at its magnetic center at all times and places, day and night.

In the postscript to the Preface, I mentioned that you are playing a part "...in the emerging spiritual science of a new level of reality." That's a lot to think about, especially the phrase *new level of reality*. However, I have a strong personal conviction that new and obviously higher levels of reality are opening to perception by human senses. What are these new levels going to tell us? They will reveal, for our understanding today, what the mystics have known for ages.

And the part *you* play? As soon as you finish reading this paragraph, please do put this book aside a few moments. Sit quietly, with a minimum of physical movement. Let your consciousness resonate with the idea of your self as a spiritual being, functioning on the plane of refined vibrational energies. Let that idea continue to float in your consciousness until you feel, even to a slight degree, a lifting sensation—a realization that you are indeed a being apart from your body but not separate from it. In that sense of partial difference between body and higher self, note your perceptions. Is there a feeling of wonderment, that a new world is opening to you? That you are at the gateway to a broader-than-ever life experience? That you are somehow sensing, and thus experiencing, new marvels of relationship between physical and spiritual levels of life?

If you have in any way been "moved" by the spirit of the above questions, I would consider it an indication that you are participating, along with others, in the new spiritual science. It is the emerging spiritual science which tomorrow will become one with the conventional physical sciences. Today it is the experimental mystical science of individuals like you and me.

Vibrations impinge upon substances that are susceptible to them. Some of those substances, such as audio and video tapes, and computer drives and disks, possess the quality of retaining those vibrations and preserving them until they are changed by other vibrations. In the same way, the vibrational essences of your life record themselves on primary substance. There, they are preserved until changed by your thoughts and acts. Changes, through electro-magnetic affinities, are entered in your personal file in primary substance. Each entry in the file is known as a *field*. We'll see what that means to you in the next section.

2

FIELD...*is an entry of a single important event of your life into your Akashic Records file. All the entries of your life combined comprise your file. A single event is entered in its own electromagnetic field within the file.*

Imagine a cave dweller during the most ancient of times. He kept records of himself and his family by drawing pictographs on the walls of his home. He recorded his prowess as a hunter, or his valor in battle. His accomplishments and his aspirations were made a somewhat permanent record with a crude yet awesome beauty that left a lasting, unique memorandum of what he was, what he did, and what he wanted to do or become.

Records, that we residents of earth still cannot accurately decipher, are contained in the gigantic Nazca lines in Peru. "Drawn" with unbelievable accuracy and size, some are only visible and appreciated from at least 1500 feet in the air. There are similar heroic sized lines on the surface of the earth near Blythe, California. Pyramids in numerous locations around the world, temples at the bottom of the sea, burial and ceremonial mounds everywhere and, in modern days, time capsules in the cornerstones of buildings, and computer files, all attest to the human passion for record keeping.

Obviously, there is an inner, forceful urge to record. And a compulsion so universal must be part and parcel of the human spirit. "As above, so below," said Hermes, the ancient messenger of Light. And that includes Records in the Akasha mode, and records on the earthly vibratory level. So humankind, in what sometimes almost amounts to a frenzy, keeps records in business, research, engineering, sports, at work and play, on and on. And now, with the computer, the activity reaches nearly unbelievable proportions. This inner compulsion is but the earthly reflection of a higher, similar activity, the Akashic Records.

As far as we have learned, the ancients didn't conceive of vibrational energies in the way we know them today. Of course there has always been electromagnetic activity in the universe, but the ancients had no computer science at their disposal, no model on which to base their concepts. Some among them wrote of a system of *recording angels*. Perhaps those angels are the equivalent of the energies we think of as electromagnetic positive and negative charges.

Ancient Angelology, Modern Records

Actually, it was assumed there were two types of angels: 1) conscious entities of a higher than human but less than Divine status, and 2) entities which were aspects of force but without individual consciousness, such as the angel of the morning, for example, representing a special type of energy predominant until high noon. The mystical Essenes engaged in conscious interaction with both types. They termed the process of association with "angelic" forces as *Angelology*.

Many ancients were convinced that the phenomenon of there being a *Book of God's Remembrance* had to involve angelic beings. They felt that the angels must have been acting on God's behalf because God was too busy to keep track of every person's thoughts and acts. Therefore, so they believed, there must have been recording angels to assist in the process.

In esoteric Judaism, recording angels closely observed the deeds of human beings and registered them in "the book." The record was usually presented at death, but could be presented earlier. In either event, it resulted in judgment (or the objectification of ripe karma) for the individual.

Many Hebrew esotericists believed that each person was accompanied through life by a recording angel, known as Metatron. He was also known by several other names: Prince of the World, Measurer of the Heavens, Prince of the Presence. It was Metatron's responsibility to help God monitor the activities of his human creations. Metatron did this by entering the deeds of each human in a special book kept in the higher dimensions. The purpose of the book was to help God make his decisions when death summoned one to the hall of judgment. However some thought there were two of the angelic recorders assigned to every individual. These two were called upon to bear witness when the person whose life they were recording entered the higher domain. The idea was that when two witnesses agreed upon a good deed, or bad, their testimony must be accurate.

In another Judaic concept, the days between Rosh Hashanah (Jewish New Year) and Yom Kippur (Day of Atonement) are special opportunities to repent of sins committed during the year and receive forgiveness for them. The proper repentance results in sins being erased from the Book of God's Remembrance. If you have sinned against God, God will forgive you if you are truly repentant.

However, if you have sinned against a person you must make it up to that person.

In Islamic tradition, the angel Gabriel is the chief recording angel. He is the one who is reputed to have written the *Koran* for Muhammad to "read" psychically and put into words. Allah's deputies included two recording angels for every person, in charge of the records of their thoughts and acts. At judgment time, one angel sat on the right hand of a person appearing before the final tribunal, the other on the left. During one's life, it was said that the angel on the right hand writes the record of a good deed ten times. When a bad act is committed, the left hand angel is requested not to record it for seven hours in case the evil doer makes immediate restitution. If the deed isn't compensated for within that period, it is entered into the record and payment is deferred until a later time.

Thus the Islamic ancients attempted to describe the process known to computer users as *R*andom *A*ccess *M*emory, or *RAM*. A computer entry is at first held in RAM temporarily. It will not be included in the file until the operator designates that it be saved, just as the left hand angel was required to wait for a time before more permanently recording an evil deed.

You are your own recording angel. However, it isn't necessary that you consciously choose to enter in your file a record of something you do. Whatever you do of sufficient intensity makes its own vibrational imprint on the file, just as a sound of enough decibels is registered on a tape recorder. And, as the cave dweller painted a pictograph of his hunting conquests so do you, on a higher level of reality, record the accomplishments of your lifetime in the Records.

It isn't so important that you perform specific acts in life. What is important is that you act from specific motivations. The inner prompts that urge you to acts worthy of registration on the Records should arise from what you are. How do you define yourself? Here's a spiritual discipline that will help you do so—help you follow those two timeless injunctions: "Know thyself," and "To thine own self, be true."

Meditate briefly on the question, "How do I define myself?" This is what you are seeking, so continue your reflections until the question becomes a potent inner urge.

Then, for a few moments, think of *what* you *are*, and write your thoughts in not more than two or three short sentences. Avoid thinking of what you *do*—it's what you *are* that's important. Think of details such as being a spirit, for example. Rewrite your thoughts daily until you're satisfied with your definition of yourself. Make your definition holistic, including body, emotions, mind and spirit, and as simple as possible.

Use your definition as a meditation prompter when experimenting with some of the ideas that follow. It will help you create the proper vibrational attunement with your own file and its fields in the Akashic Records.

Our present understanding offers us the illustration of a modern device, the computer, capable of receiving and storing signals which represent information. The electromagnetic signals generated through your thoughts and acts are stored in the receptive, sensitive aspects of primary substance to become your personal cosmic Akashic Record. The process for adding new facts to your personal field may be compared to the computer process known as *input*.

3

INPUT...*What you think and do is electro-*
magnetically registered or "recorded" in your
Akashic Record. It all adds to the fields in
your personal file.

As I type these words on my computer keyboard, I'm mechanically and electromagnetically inputting details to a file I've named AKASHIC.BK, which distinguishes it from all other files in the computer.

During the life of this manuscript many changes will be made. There will be daily deletions and corrections of old material—and a large amount of new information input. The same process occurs in your relationship with the Records. The "name" of your file is what you are in life. Deletions, corrections and the addition of new information to your file never ceases.

On your journey through earth life, you've become involved in a series of events that are extremely meaningful to you—as opposed to incidents which are less meaningful, and which quickly fade from memory in the mists of time. Those events which contributed to your growth philosophically and spiritually are more highly charged with electromagnetic energies than others, and are indelibly recorded in your personal Akashic Record.

We "network" with each other, and with all forms of life, often without realizing it on a conscious level. Then, even years later, the impact of such experiences strikes us with the power of a lightning flash and we wonder why our realization arrived so tardily at the mental terminal. One such insight came to me more than half a century behind schedule. I'm passing it on to you for a special purpose which I'll explain later.

You've probably already decided that I entertain some pretty unusual ideas. Truth is, the pattern of my belief system is wilder than a Christmas necktie. The story begins at my birth when my grandfather planted a cherry tree in his backyard. He did it as a more or less humorous compliance with an old "superstition." Yet I now wonder if he wasn't more serious than he allowed anyone to know. The old custom was that if you plant a tree at the birth of a child, the tree will always reflect the state of that child wherever he or she might be. There was a "superstitious" belief that the life of child and tree were mysteriously and invisibly connected.

In later years I was told the tree first struggled to stay alive, as I did. And that grandpa struggled on behalf of both tree and me. Then as the tree really took root and developed, so I, too, became healthy and stronger.

The thrill of achieving enough nerve to overcome my fear as a five-year-old and climb the lowest branches of that tree nestles still in my memory as one of my first accomplishments. Later I picked cherries by the boxful and sold them from a little red wagon all along Lincolnway East in LaPorte, Indiana. Years later, when the property was sold and the new owners felled the tree to erect a building, I felt "uneasy" for weeks. It didn't occur to me then, but I now believe that the cherry tree and I shared a long energy relationship.

Please do put this book down for a few moments, think of a time when an experience of a similar nature has occurred in your life. For a few moments give reign to its resonance and meaning in your consciousness. Then consider that this same kind of energy interchange also occurs between you and *higher* life forms. And between you and the Akashic Records.

Now I ask you to consider that when you pass under a tree, though you say not a word, it hears you speak. The silent voice of your entire being falls within the field of the tree's primitive form of consciousness and announces your presence, your life energy, perhaps even your emotions and thoughts. And if you will but listen with your own inner auditory mechanism, you may "hear" the tree give you some good advice. It may tell you to be placid and allow your own natural growth to occur. It may suggest that you, too, have roots, both in the earth and in the heavens. It may remind you that you can be refreshed and invigorated by the spiritual waters and the spiritual light—and that you possess the capacity to outgrow yourself over and over throughout a lifetime. It's no wonder the ancients held their trees holy and sacred.

Thus the tree incorporates something of your personality within itself, and you incorporate something of the tree's nature within yourself. This kind of energy interchange is constantly occurring between you and all forms of life, not excluding any of them.

You now engage in, always have and always will, an energy exchange "conversation" with primary substance. What is being said in that conversation is usually not known on the level of your normal consciousness. It's perceived, so

I believe, on vibrational levels both above and below that everyday segment of your being which is dominant during your present incarnation. The segment of your being which has both roots and antennae—the roots for drawing *up* important physical level qualities, and antennae for drawing *in* even more important spiritual level traits. Or you may wish to consider the allegory in its opposite form, as did many of the ancients—trunks, branches and leaves of the human tree in the earth, roots in the air. Draw sustenance through roots in the higher planes for expression through branches and foliage in the lower.

Is My Present Name on the Records?

Your *name* in the Akashic Records is not the given name conferred upon you by parents or the name of the family into which you were born. Consider that when it is said, following a prayer, "We ask this in the name of the Christ," it is not intended, as many believe, to be a literal statement. What actually is meant is, "We ask this in the nature of, or in the Spirit of, the Christ." When an aspirant undergoes an initiation, symbolic of the attainment of a greater degree of understanding, the change in that person's nature is recognized and symbolized by a change in name. Thus, for example, Saul became Paul. This outer change represents the inner.

Your true name is *what* you are, not *who* you are!

Your true name, your nature, is the composite of all the electromagnetic qualities you express. In this sense, among even billions of people there are no two names alike. The shades of interests and their duration, personality and its variations, soul intensity and its mental and spiritual evolvement, and thousands of other factors, determine the individuality and uniqueness of your name, or the total magnetic reality of your being, in the Records.

Ralph Waldo Emerson long ago wrote, "A man is a center for nature, running out threads of relation through every thing, fluid and solid, material and elemental." Was he not saying that what you think and do flows into the universe of primal energies?

If what you are thinking at this moment happens for some reason to be specially meaningful to you, if it creates a lifelong modification of your thought and action patterns, you are not the same person you were a few moments ago. In the esoteric sense, your name has changed because you've become a different person. You've changed the "threads of relation" between you and all the rest of life. As that different person, your input into your Akashic Record reflects the change in you. It remains *your* exclusive record.

Is my *every* act on record for all eternity?

When I criticize the sales person in a store, is it registered on the Akashic Records? Only if my act reflects a prevailing and continuing attitude in my mind. If it does, my act simply reinforces the "messages" of a similar nature I've already placed on the Records. Is it unusual for me to be critical? Or am I frequently expressing a critical, cynical attitude toward others and life in general? Or is such a life mode contrary to my predominating attitude, my "name"? What prevails on earth prevails in a higher dimension.

Emerson's "threads of relation" find and strengthen each other on every level. They affect responsive cells of the human body as well as the Records. Emerson suggested that "...like can only be known by like." In other words, similar vibrational energies respond only to similar vibrational energies—as do two C strings on a harp, even though octaves apart. In their response mode they contribute to each others' influence. Over time, thought patterns can either destroy or strengthen your body. Same thought patterns increase the longevity and forcefulness of same thought patterns. Truth on the physical level is also truth on the cosmic. So, repeated thought patterns, for better or worse, are registered on the Akashic Records. They are the Input that you are repeating, revitalizing and reinforcing.

There's another result of thought patterns which is accepted by many esotericists. It's based on the principle of the three seed atoms—three atoms of an etheric nature through which you maintain your contact with life's physical level through a series of incarnations.

One of these micro-vibrational particles, known as the physical seed atom, is located during physical life at the core of the heart energy center. Its nature causes it to resonate with body energies. The second seed atom is known as the emotional seed atom, residing deep in the solar plexus energy center and resonating with emotional energies. The third, the mental seed atom, is lodged during your physical life in the pituitary/pineal center, often known as the Third Eye center. It resonates with all the energies of your consciousness.

The integrated energies of your thoughts, emotions and physical acts are constantly impinging upon these three seed atoms. Their collective vibrational essence represents the principal aspects of your entire being. They become specially effective networkers with your Akashic Record.

In a period of repose you may find it possible to "connect" with the physical seed atom in your heart. To the best of your ability, sense that you are mentally carrying that physical atom to the emotional seed atom centered in your solar plexus area. There the two vibrational essences unite harmoniously as though they were two notes of a musical chord. Then inwardly carry that chord, the vibrations of the physical and emotional seed atoms, to the pineal/pituitary center and combine them with the mental seed atom in an even more beautiful chord. Finally, mentally take this chord into a higher vibratory level, the domain of spiritual life, close to the level of primary substance. You have used your "name," or the nature of your entire being as expressed by the combined seed atoms, as the password for opening your Akashic Record. And you've increased the possibility of receiving helpful information from them.

4

OUTPUT..._The material which your thoughts and acts enter in your Akashic Record file is "played back" to you in a variety of ways._

The Gospel story is that a farmer went forth to sow—some of the results pleased him; some didn't. Evidently he wasn't a very careful or selective farmer. He cast valuable seeds on stony ground where sun and birds destroyed them. He threw seeds among the thorns which choked the seedlings to death. But some seeds he cast upon good ground where they grew and repaid the farmer with a bountiful harvest.

This simple story is one of the great illustrations of a principle that leads to success in life. It may be applied to success in a marriage or other relationship, to success in business, success in spiritual evolvement, or any other kind of achievement you might imagine. What kind of seeds do you sow, and where do you sow them? These are important questions to ask yourself.

The story also applies to the Akashic Records, and our comparison of those Records to the computer you may have used today. Early in its existence the computer industry was sometimes faced with a program that seemed to generate output loaded with "inexplicable errors." This output soon earned the label "garbage."

With the realization that what emerged from the computer had to be in perfect response to the user's commands, a new phrase was added to our language: "Garbage in, garbage out." It meant that whatever emerged from the computer perfectly reflected whatever was entered. As the law of gravity notes that "what goes up must come down," the principle of computer science recognizes that "the accuracy of the printer's output depends on the accuracy of the operator's original input." What comes out through the printer must be the same message as the operator entered, including flaws and errors.

Now it's sometimes comforting and sometimes irritating to realize that the outside agency (the computer) cannot necessarily fix what the operator enters. The human being is still responsible for the message. Output accurately reflects input. The same is true of the vibrational relationship between a human being and the Akashic Records. As a matter of fact, isn't the same true of all life? The Records will play back (as does a tape recorder), exactly what is put in. "As you sow, so shall you reap."

At this point we're involved with concepts far more remarkable than the greatest computer ever created. We're dealing with cosmic concepts, eternal verities, relating to the ebb and flow of life on a cosmic scale. For a few pages we'll span time and space with our minds and perhaps arrive at a revelation of the ways in which you relate to mortality, infinity and Divinity.

Occasional, spontaneous contacts with the Akashic Records could be compared with the output of information from a computer file. My first realization of this came as a result of comparing an unusual personal experience many years ago with my present limited knowledge of modern computer science.

In 1933, I visited the Chicago World's Fair with a few friends. On one occasion we decided each of us would go our separate ways for the day. In the heat and mugginess of a Chicago August day, I wandered aimlessly past buildings containing exhibits from countries around the world. Suddenly I found myself pausing before a large building housing the Italian exhibit. Never having had any interest in Italy, I wondered why I found myself entering the building.

Just inside the entrance I saw a large, rusty, ship's anchor, held upright on a rack. It was behind a rope barricade prohibiting visitors from approaching too close to the displays. I noted a sign which read, "Please do not touch the anchor." Of course I leaned over the barricade and placed my palm flat against the anchor's surface.

At that moment, I lost consciousness of my surroundings. Chicago's summer heat was no longer oppressive. In fact, the building and the crowds of people entirely disappeared. But I was conscious in another time and place. It was nighttime. I was aware of soft lights and festive music, mingled with the sounds of happy voices. Obviously I was observing a celebration.

But I was hiding in the shadows on the deck of a floating vessel, just outside the circle of dim lights, pressing my back against the anchor. And I realized I should not be there, for I was out of my element. I was a seaman, a slave, and I should not have been watching my superiors.

As I attempted to push further back against the anchor, into the shadows, I was suddenly aware of an approaching figure. I was terrified at the probability that I had been discovered in a place where I had no right to be, and thoughts of severe punishment horrified me. At that moment, as my terror reached a peak, my consciousness returned to Chicago again, in the Italian exhibit building, withdrawing my hand from its contact with the anchor.

The experience, which could have lasted only a few seconds, left me with complex emotions. I knew nothing of such experiences. I was startled, and tried to dismiss the event as though it were merely some curious irrationality. But the reality of it persisted. I walked further into the building to the next object in the exhibit and read the sign explaining that it was a pleasure barge, several hundred years old. The barge and anchor were found on the bottom of a mountain lake which had been drained for their removal. The barge and its anchor were used by Italian royalty of that time as a place for private parties.

Was I momentarily in touch with a previous life? Had I long ago left on the anchor a powerful vibrational imprint which had been reinforced by my terror at that moment? Did the Chicago contact with the anchor activate the retrieval of a personal message unknowingly left on the Akashic Records several hundred years ago? And did that message ultimately drastically change my life? I believe it did, for it was not long after that experience that my life seemed almost automatically to turn toward esoteric and mystical teachings. And after a few years of concentrated studies I left the business world to become a teacher in this field.

Was all this the result of a vibrational injection of my dharma into my current incarnation? Were the Akashic Records "outputting" influences that would in time make it possible for me to change the course of my life? And was this occurring at the first time in my life when I would be receptive to such a drastic change? It is only through writing this book that I have come to see this possibility with clarity and intensity of belief. For me this event very obviously (as

I viewed it later) marked the beginning of a turning point in my life. I now can see the evolvement of destiny, sense of mission, responsibility and satisfaction (a special kind of happiness) beginning at that point, which had not previously ever been experienced. My dharma was vigorously released from latency in the Records into everyday activity.

And I further believe that you will be able to make this same application with one or more occurrences in your life experience. We do not know when events of the past may come flowing into the consciousness of our present lives as door openers to future growth.

We are all subject to subtle vibrational energies, but we aren't always receptive to them. Sometimes timing and preparation aren't in place. The output or playback, from the Akashic Records doubtless sends many messages to us that either we do not receive or we simply ignore. This is not to say that every sudden whim is a prompt from the Records. We are in the early stages of the special kind of inner sensitizing that enables us to become attuned to the Records. We need to continue developing that sensitivity to retrieve (or recognize) the meaning of their energies, just as a person with perfect pitch recognizes the scale designation of a musical note when it is sounded.

The Records Help Fulfill Your Dharma and Karma

The Hindu philosophers express dharma and karma as consciousness states that become objectified in individual human lives. We do not always understand them. It is true that, as the Christian says, "God works in mysterious ways, His wonders to perform." Even when, with visible clarity, we view the circumstances of our lives, we are not always competent in connecting them precisely with their causes.

Dharma is a Sanskrit word to which, through the ages,

numerous meanings have been assigned. Literally, the word means *cosmic order* or *law*. Its use is prevalent in the Hindu and Buddhist disciplines. It is related to natural and ethical principles that apply to everyone, regardless of religious beliefs, and to practices which lead to observance of a higher law and attainment of a higher life.

Among additional meanings of the word dharma are the concepts of *destiny*, *reward*, *happiness*, *responsibility*, and *the creation of good* in one's life. Some teachers insist upon the application of one meaning only. I suggest that all the meanings are valuable and useful to the seeker of spiritual unfoldment.

Whatever your choice of meaning for the word, dharma is involved in the Akashic Record output in your life. The goals of your higher self have been infused into the Records. There are rare and wonderful occasions, when circumstances and conditions are appropriate, when the influence of the Records filters down through the vibrational layers of primary substance and is "output" into your life in a dramatic manner.

One type of more or less automatic Akashic Records output, then, is dharma; a second type is *karma*. Karma is another Sanskrit word. It pertains to the consequences of *a deed*, *an act*, or *the outpouring of "fate."* It is more closely connected with the mundane aspects of life regarding earthly responsibilities—rewards for good and penalties for wrongdoing. "As you sow, so shall you reap."

In the Hindu and Buddhist philosophies particularly, karma is the total and ongoing result of a person's thoughts and actions through successive incarnations. Karma, as it is output into your life, may be the distasteful result of an improper act. But always remember that it may also be the reward for a good deed. Never judge karma by its outer appearance. Figuratively speaking, today's action is tomorrow's karma, pleasant or unpleasant.

That statement is true in a literal as well as a figurative sense. However, in the practice of speculative spirituality leading to an inner realization of truth, one's view must include a time span much longer than a mere 24 hours. We're discussing a concept of something that must have existed since before the beginning—that is before the beginning which we can imagine under the limitations of conventional theory.

So, we're confronted with questions, and we must use our spiritual sensitivities to speculate upon the answers.

The first question is, "From our *earthly perspective*, in the complexity of creation why need there be Akashic Records?" The second question is, "And from the *higher perspective*, why would they exist?"

Answers from the earthly perspective are:

First, because the Records serve the purpose of helping individuals, such as you and me, evaluate our lives. When we come face to face with the messages on the Records, in an understandable format, they help us see our own larger life and evaluate it in a totally different context than the normal physical life span. In doing so we gain a previously unavailable perspective for our progress from incarnation to incarnation.

Second, the Records explain those aspects of karma that are unclear, or which seem unfair to us. The question, "Why did God do this to me?" has no answer, for God did not do it. If it is changed to, "Why and how did this situation come to exist?" we have at least the opportunity of arriving at solutions to the many personal puzzles that life seems to present.

Third, the Records help us set goals for progress in this and future incarnations. Repeating errors in a different way isn't really gaining any ground. It simply reinforces the status quo. There is no evolvement. But when we can become aware of the underlying factors of past events we can specifically set goals that help us overcome our deficiencies and attain the inner development of which we are capable.

The above ideas are in answer to the first question regarding why there are Akashic Records—from the normal point of view.

Now here is a spiritually speculative answer from a higher viewpoint:

The Records exist because, due to the normal and natural interaction of energies between the individual human being, and the energies of cosmic and eternal life, the existence of the Records could not be avoided. Divine Consciousness could not do otherwise. In a Plan too awesome for us to grasp easily at this point in our evolvement, there simply is no other way for the progress and continuum of life to be conducted on a basis that is *available* and *fair to each person*—each person who is also a living cell in this great organism of the universe.

Dharma and Karma are two automatic, continuous retrieval aspects of the Akashic Records. There are other aspects—some of them integrated into the processes we think of as birth and death, and some we designate as "reading" the Records, which we accomplish through a deliberately created state of consciousness. In our computer analogy, we would think of it as *retrieval*.

5

RETRIEVE...a word that describes the process of getting in touch with your file in the Akashic Records, or one of its fields, for the purpose of understanding major events in your life, and their meaning to you.

Jesus said "...rejoice because your names are written in heaven." To what was he referring? Is there a simple list of names? Or is there a record of meaningful activities that can be retrieved? Surely he spoke on a level more significant, and a subject more profound, than a mere list of names!

You probably have had many physical incarnation names, acquired through the centuries. Is there a way you are designated in the Akashic Records? Are you listed in the Book of God's Remembrance? Might not God have said, "I shall make human beings in my image, but I shall make no two alike, and in that way shall I distinguish one from another." You are the product of neither mold nor chemical, but of a creative wellspring whose components are constantly in a state of remodeling as they pass through an ever changing material and spiritual environment.

The subtle energy differences between one person and

another are like cosmic fingerprints, or DNA differences, between individuals. Vibrational dissimilarities are the differing characteristics that distinguish your individuality from all others. These distinctions set your Record apart, and knowing something about them is one of the steps toward your being able to retrieve from it important information about yourself.

According to a physician, Levi Dowling, M.D., as well as many others, there *is* a record which can be retrieved. Dr. Dowling, an ordained minister, as well as a medical doctor and a publisher of Sunday School material, wrote a book titled *The Aquarian Gospel of Jesus the Christ*. It was originally published in 1908 and is still being published today. The book is the story of the life of Jesus, including the years that are entirely omitted from the traditional accounts in the Gospels.

Dowling did not write the book out of his own consciousness. Each morning between the hours of two and six o'clock he entered a period of absolute silence, and in that totally quiescent, trance-like state became mentally, psychically and spiritually attuned to the Akashic Records. The messages he gleaned from them became the remarkable book, *The Aquarian Gospel*. Dowling's work is considered by many as evidence of the existence of the Akashic Records and the possibility of "reading" them. No claim is made that Dowling's book is accurate in every detail—in any type of communication, some inaccuracies are bound to occur. The book does answer many questions for the serious student of Jesus' life.

Consideration of the Akashic Records raises the question of reincarnation. Do we pass through physical life more than once, hopefully rectifying errors on each occasion and gaining new wisdom?

Yes, I believe we do. And as part of the process, I believe there are two special occasions when you experience a personal contact with your file in the Akashic Records. One occurrence is just prior to your leaving the higher world for re-entry into this physical domain. It's a time when you gather into your personal and unique vibrational being all the elements which you wish to use during incarnation. It's such an important event that many mystics think of it as a special spiritual initiation. You don't simply swish into the physical form your parents prepared for you. You are assisted by a spiritual plane "practitioner" who helps you create a retrieval mode of consciousness in contact with your personal Akashic Record file. Through that contact you determine which of any leftover debts you wish to clear away; which talents you wish to develop; which lessons will contribute to your growth. With this knowledge you make decisions regarding the environments and sometimes even major events you wish to experience during your approaching lifetime on earth. You may even be involved in the choice of your parents as part of fulfilling the purposes for which you are earth destined.

The second time you contact your personal Record file is when you pass through the process of putting aside your physical body to enter the light of higher dimensions at death. Once again a higher level "practitioner" of the art helps you gain insights to the earthly episode you've just experienced and entered into your file. Accomplishments and ineptitudes are retrieved from your file and examined to help you evaluate your "performance" here on this earthly level. And to help you understand the reasons for many of the major (and sometimes traumatic) incidents you have experienced.

Do you think you will have no interest in these two

special occasions? Probably more than you realize as you read this. One of the most distinctive characteristics of the human being is that, of all the animal families, the human is probably the only one interested in record keeping. There must be a reason for this (as there is for all things) and the reason must be related to your spiritual evolvement.

So we aren't amiss to presume that these two retrieval episodes of Akashic Record contact constitute our getting in touch with our "names" as they are "written in heaven." In other words, when we make the contact at birth and death we are, on a higher level of reality, in touch with the complete nature of ourselves as they exist in that moment. Remember that in Section Three of this work it was pointed out that "your true name is *what* you are, not *who* you are." These birth and death episodes with the Records help you learn, on a higher level of your consciousness, *what* you are.

Find Purpose in Life

Emerson wrote: "We are piqued to some purpose."

Piqued—not a commonly used word. However I think it appropriately describes the nature of most person's interest in the Akashic Records. Being piqued occasionally is the stuff esotericists and mystics are made of.

Piqued—a kind of annoying, sometimes aggravating, nagging impulse to want to know more of something that can barely be known. Esotericists and mystics are piqued. They search for the answers to life's puzzles and riddles. Their unorthodox search isn't confined to conventional concepts, to textbooks and encyclopedias, or attendance at seminars, helpful as all these may be. Their search is conducted through higher levels of the self, consideration of the non-conventional, and on journeys into vibratory dimensions of which we are all a part, but of which we usually gain only an occasional glimpse. From time to time, your interest in the Akashic Records will be piqued.

Shortly after I first read Emerson's brief but meaningful sentence about being piqued, I met a friend of several years, a quite well-to-do retired businessman in his eighties. He lamented his growing concern that somehow the purpose of his life had escaped him. His disappointment at this loss was so great, and so touching, that it literally permeated the atmosphere with an aura of sadness. I shared his hurt, but couldn't help him for, as good a person as he was, he was not the kind to be piqued concerning the eternal spiritual verities. The focus of his life, leading to his disappointment with it, was limited to truths and concepts of the temporal variety.

How dismaying it is to feel that life is shallow and meaningless. But what a tremendously satisfying experience it is to discover that suddenly your consciousness views a broader vista than ever before. That you are seeing vertically as well as horizontally. It's almost as if you've learned another language and gained admission to another country and its interesting people.

A recognized Akashic Record retrieval experience opens just such a new and greater understanding of your own life. It's definitely a mystical experience. You cannot fully describe it, for its vista and vocabulary are of another dimension. The language of Spirit is seldom comfortable or even recognizable on the human tongue. Because such experiences so rarely occur, and in their purest form are so difficult to attain, it seems almost as though Divine Intelligence hid them from human finding. But ever before us is the challenging statement: "...there is nothing covered, that shall not be revealed; and hid, that shall not be known."

Several times I've been in Egypt in the presence of

esoteric Egyptologists who have pointed out that in hieroglyphics and tomb decorations there are occasional representations of Egyptian headdresses which have the appearance of being highly specialized antennae. Other works of Egyptian art depict a person holding what appears to be a device in exactly the same shape as an oversize tuning fork. Some believe these objects are remnants of Atlantean era instruments used for tuning in with extremely high level wavelengths. Many believe they are devices for capturing the frequencies broadcast from outer space. And others accept the idea that these articles, bearing a startling similarity to modern high frequency antennae, may have been for the purpose of attunement to the Akashic Records on behalf of the pharaoh to aid him in governing the kingdom.

Modern science has an astonishing facility for overlooking what seem to be the wildest fantasies of "science fiction," and then surpassing them. It required a comparatively long time to outdo Captain Nemo and his submarine, but hardly any time at all to outdistance Dick Tracy's wrist radio. One day, perhaps not too far distant, you may be able to retrieve to a TV screen in your living room, or shrine, a recapitulation of your major life events, called in through your home computer for your viewing and analysis.

Now let's do some "supposing" for a moment. Perhaps the ideas expressed above are too "far out" to be acceptable. In that case we can only accept whatever exists in our lives as practically unchangeable, and remain depressed or at least unfulfilled as did the friend I previously described. Or we can accept the "science fiction" theory that there is a distinct path from subjective imagination to objective reality. The theory is that somewhere and somehow the wildest dreams are pregnant with the sperm of that reality, waiting to be born into the everyday world we temporarily inhabit.

Let us now leap from one kind of reality to another— from the reality of a Biblical record of a miraculous event to the reality of that same record as a metaphysical and mystical allegory.

The story background: King Bel-Shazzar made a great feast for a thousand of his principal subjects. His father had robbed the temple of its gold and silver dishes, and they were being used to serve the banquet, a sign of contempt for the spiritual thought of a conquered people. In addition, praise was expressed for the gods of gold and other precious metals.

The drama: "In the same hour came forth fingers of a man's hand, and wrote over against the candlestick upon the plaster of the wall of the king's palace, and the king saw part of the hand that wrote.

"Then the king's countenance was changed, and his thoughts troubled him, so that the joints of his loins were loosed, and his knees smote one against another."

The king then brought to the banquet room all the wise men of Babylon and promised them great rewards for interpreting the handwriting on the wall. They all failed, for their lack of spirituality prevented them from understanding the phenomenon.

At this point, the queen entered the banquet hall. Note that from the esoteric view there is now added the feminine element to the predominantly masculine polarization existing up to that moment. It can easily be assumed that the queen's presence calmed the revelry and caused a more meditative approach to the remarkable occurrence taking place.

The solution: The queen suggested that Daniel, "...in whom is the spirit of the holy gods...and understanding and wisdom..." be brought to interpret the writing. The king ordered that it be done. Note that now the essence of higher spirituality, wisdom and understanding is being brought into the mysterious situation.

The conclusion: Daniel refused the king's offer of great material rewards and agreed to interpret the phenomenon. He told the king that God sent the hand and the writing was from Him. "It is telling you", said Daniel, "that God has numbered your kingdom and finished it. That you are weighed in the balances, and found wanting. And that the kingdom will be divided among the Medes and Persians." That night, the king was slain and his kingdom taken by his enemies.

The allegory: The energy of what appeared to be a hand, writing on the wall, came from higher dimensions, projected from Bel-Shazzar's Akashic Records. In the mystical language of the higher realms his roots vibrationally reflected the nature of his life, and indicated the future toward which it was progressing. All this could be accomplished only when the proper balance of masculine and feminine energies prevailed in the banquet hall, and when the spiritualizing agency in the form of Daniel was also present.

The event in this allegory was a spontaneous occurrence. Bel-Shazzar's karmic playback from his Record was intense and concentrated. For reasons beyond our present understanding, this is not always the case. There are instances when the automatic, spontaneous playback of the Record occurs over a longer time. There are other situations in which one consciously wishes to gain helpful insight into a purposeful life. Retrieval from the Records is then accomplished through a deliberate effort to make the contact. How is it accomplished? Here, and in other sections of this book, you are being given a number of ways to get in touch with the Records.

How to Get in Touch with the Records

In the Bel-Shazzar allegory, there is indicated for us some of the requirements for the retrieval of information from the Akashic Records. First is a proper balancing of all vibrational factors. It's important that sensitive psychic receptivity not be disturbed by physical, emotional or mental distress—balance throughout one's inner life is a necessity, at least during the time an attempt is made to contact the Records.

Pure intention of purpose is another requisite. Admission into the higher vibratory realms is not to be undertaken lightly. Many of the ancients symbolized this by creating a space for a "holy of holies," which could be entered without disastrous results only by a high priest. One's "password" for coming in touch with the Records is one's name—and remember that your name in the Akashic Records is the complete profile of your predominating nature. Your name is *what* you are.

A personal contact with your file in the Records may make it possible for you to gain information helpful in accomplishing the purposes of your present life. In esoteric lore, it has always been accepted that the high vibratory nature of the primary substance in which the Records are located is beyond the sensory range of the human being. And that our human contact is made with a lower vibratory range of energies known as the *mental reflecting ethers*.

It has also been accepted that these mental reflecting ethers do not always perfectly mirror the data residing in primary substance, any more than the physical body perfectly reflects the spirit residing in it. Therefore, any information acquired through this process must be accepted with logical reservations as to its absolute accuracy.

Can others contact the Records on your behalf and give you accurate information regarding their contents and meaning? Yes, with the same limitations mentioned above, and some advantages, too. A person whose psychic abilities are oriented toward contacting the Records may be able to do so more quickly and accurately than you, due to greater experience. This may not be true for everyone, and certainly the same reservations and requirements for the use of logic should be observed.

Another person contacts the Records by means of consciously or nonconsciously first becoming engrossed in sensing your predominant nature, through empathy with your presence. This creates in that person the vibrational key that allows access to your file in the Records.

What about aspects of your life which you wish to have kept as secrets? They are not available to another person as long as the idea of keeping them secret intensely pervades your own nature. In everyone's life there exists what we each think of as private information, known only to ourselves, and public information which we don't mind others knowing. The latter is the kind which a "reader" of the Records would find available.

A Technique for Contacting the Records

If you are attempting to contact the Records on your own behalf, you should be able to come closer to the primary source than anyone else. The possible limitation here is that probably you would not be as practiced at it, and would not be able to do it as well. The advantage is that, when you do accomplish it, you have access to more information, the private type, than does the general "reader."

The meditation technique: When a computer user creates a file which is confidential in nature, a "password" is created so that only someone who knows it can retrieve that file. Your password is your name, as you've already read. So for you to activate this password and gain entrance to your file, you need to begin by quietly creating a harmonious inner state of consciousness. The inner state you achieve reflects your attitudinal preparation for the steps to follow.

Drift easily into an intense meditative state, making certain your consciousness is free of either ego-centered or self-judgmental thoughts, that your emotions are calm, that your body is at ease. You are creating the password, the vibrational affinity, that attunes you to your file in the Akashic Records. You are finding your self on this level and merging it with the Record of your Self on the higher level.

You may apply any meditational technique you've already found helpful to further stabilize your inner calmness and strengthen your connection with higher vibrational energies.

If this "finding" yourself is accomplished properly, you are apt to feel a somewhat floating sensation. It isn't that you leave your body astrally; you simply have the sensation of being weightless. Hold that thought in your mind a few moments.

Then, try to think of yourself as a whole being—body, emotions, mind, spirit, past, present, oncoming future—all fused and synthesized into one spiritualized entity, ready to accept sensations from a higher source. These sensations temporarily become one with you, and in the process supply your consciousness with information enabling you to examine, evaluate and apply it to your life.

The query: If you can manage to do so without disturbing your serenity, quietly, slowly, inwardly ask questions. It is possible that inner answers will emerge from the higher source you are contacting, giving further information of value.

"What kind of questions should I ask?" Here are some suggestions. But to keep this complex and difficult experience as simple as possible, ask only one question per session.

> What is the basis for my present situation and why am I in it?
> What is the lesson I can learn from it?
> What are my present relationships teaching me?
> What are the negative personal characteristics in my life now?
> What are my positive personal characteristics which I should work to strengthen?
> For my personal growth, which of my individual characteristics should I begin to change?

You may have other questions of importance. Remember this experience is not for dealing with trivialities. You are seeking the relationship between you and the cosmos.

The response: How do answers to your query arrive in your consciousness? Sometimes in exceptionally strong feelings. Or inner visions. Even occasionally in what seem to be actual spoken words, discerned with an inner auditory mechanism not connected with your normal audio passageways.

Whatever the method of response, the message is the important factor. When you believe you've received such a communication, it is important to test it first by writing it.

Read what you've written and see whether or not your own immediate reaction is favorable. Do you interiorly accept it as truth for you? Be certain. To leap to conclusions because you *want* them to be true, rather than because they *are* true may lead to consequences you'd prefer not to experience. You must be the judge.

The absorption: Give yourself a waiting period to absorb any inner experience you may have. Allow the various energies you've encountered to resonate through your consciousness, without attaching meaning to them at this time. This is an important factor in the process. It provides you with an opportunity to sort out elements that may be unrelated to your search. You might well wish to consider this part of the process as a time for living with your self, or your Self.

Write a memo to your self about your experiences; live with it for at least twenty-four hours. Rewrite it several times if you wish, for improving both the message and its clarity. Then decide whether or not it is valid for your further exploration.

The analysis: Analysis of your message may be the most difficult element of your experience. The opportunity to mislead yourself is present though hidden. But if changes have been indicated as the result of your search, you must at least consider them. They are valueless if they lead to action but no action is taken.

Continue to examine your memo(s) to your self. What action is indicated? Again, a series of questions proposed to your own inner nature helps this part of the process.

For example, if your question as listed in the section captioned **The query** was, "What is the basis for my present situation?" then you must decide what you are going to do about the responses you received. You need to decide what *you* are going to do to change the basis for your situation. What action on your part is called for?

You have four inner levels of life on which you can make changes in response to any question you've asked: physical, emotional, mental and spiritual. In addition, you can also act to make changes in the external aspects of your life. You can create changes in personal, social, and business relationships as well as many other influential situations in your life.

The computer user studies what has been input and retrieved, and decides what improvements may result from editing and changing. And your analysis of what to do as a result of your contact with the Akashic Records is quite apt to suggest changes in your life. They may be only one or two of those suggested above, or they may include several of them—and probably others as well. You are your own best editor.

Future sections include additional methods for getting in touch with your personal file in the Akashic Records.

6

EDIT...to examine and rearrange or otherwise revise through changes in various details. Editor: one who edits a newspaper or periodical, supervises and sets policy.

If you will think carefully about your life to this moment, you'll realize there's a story in it. Perhaps you've at some time thought about writing an autobiography. You may be surprised to learn that is exactly what you are doing, moment by moment, experience by experience, as you "write" your story in the Book of Remembrance.

You write your life story, as does every person, on the basic elements of space, time and eternity: primary substance—the fields in your file in the Akashic Records. And, as you enter the file in your computer, make changes, or edit it, revise, or rearrange it, so do you continue the computer analogy by being not only the author but also the editor of your life story.

"What is so special about my life?" Possibly you're asking the question at this very moment. First of all it's *yours*, and the only one you have at the moment. How could it be more special than that? Your life is unique, one of a kind in the universe. Emerson told us this in one of his earliest books when he wrote, "...you are you, and I am I, and so we remain." Without elaborating upon it he said that there's a secret strength in the law of individuality. That strength, so I believe, is immediately reinforced when you accept the concept of your uniqueness without being egotistical. It is then that you know that no one can do *precisely* what you can do; no one knows *exactly* what you know; no one is prepared to *begin and end a given day* at the same spiritual or other levels you do. So be supported, renewed and energized by the realization of your absolute individuality.

But what of the universal inner urge for connectedness? Isn't it true that, but for a few rare exceptions, we human beings want to be in contact with others, and have I not written that universal urges in the human being are reflections of similar energies of a higher nature? There are meaningful similarities in our lives in spite of the differences. You are an individual, as am I, yet together we can find relationships and connections that help us both, that give us the opportunity to express love and share other important qualities.

Your life touches other lives, and theirs touch yours. But remember that connection is not limited to earthly relationships. There is individual connection with life energies of many types. There is connection with numerous levels of life, both on earth and in higher dimensions. So when I write of individuality, I do not imply separateness, for there is no such thing.

So even though your unique life is very special, can it not be improved through your connection with the Records? Can you not be the editor and do some rearranging and revising? And remember the important fact: *the editor supervises and sets policy.*

Honestly, now, is that true in your life? You're not privileged to be "the editor" in anyone else's life. But are you truly fulfilling that function in your own?

Probably no one of us can honestly and fully answer yes to that question, for we find the need to make accommodations with others by yielding the editorial privilege to a certain extent, out of courtesy, or love, or for other reasons. But I maintain that in most major ways you and I should be the editors of our lives to the fullest possible magnitude. We should supervise and set policy.

We've already considered the concept that we are responsible for our lives, and that whatever we do with them automatically becomes registered upon the Records. Sometimes new information is registered. Sometimes old and karmically fulfilled data is deleted. It is the spiritual corollary of the edit function on your computer. With the Records the process is the simple result of induction, as when the current in one electrical wire is to a degree transmitted to another wire, even though the second wire is not connected to anything. In other words, your vibrational nature is inducted into your file in the Akashic Records. No thought upon your part is required. It's an automatic process.

This is the Age of Higher Energies

Thus the policy setting and supervision you employ in your life—your selection of motives for your acts and predominant patterns of thought—become entries in the Book of Remembrance. Is there any special practice in which you might engage which would influence this activity, and would create a stronger affinity between you and your personal page in the Records?

In the Aquarian Age we're entering, the age of mind over matter (and energy is matter), advanced seekers are becoming more and more attuned to the higher energies and a working relationship with them. It's a reorientation of conscious awareness from wanting others to do for me what I can do for myself. This is not to minimize the importance of higher influences and what they may accomplish on your behalf. It's to increase your cooperative participation with those persons and vital energies residing in higher levels of life.

So you may consider it important to enhance, or establish, a working relationship, on a deliberately conscious basis, with one of the highest energies, Biblically symbolized in the words, "And God said, Let there be light: and there was light. And God saw the light, that it was good...." Light, therefore, may be considered a vibrational energy range just a step or so below primary substance. In its lower range it is visible to our eyes. In its higher ranges it possesses a greater affinity for our minds and inner visualization techniques than for our sense of sight.

Mind, and its capacity for visualization, is a wonderful tool for enhancing life in general, and possesses a particular capacity for attunement to the Akashic Records through the energy of light. Very probably you are already familiar with light visualization techniques, and with methods for mentally directing higher light energies for specific purposes such as healing, strengthening and protection.

In brief, visualizing a sphere of light creates a thought form which contains the characteristics imparted to it by the nature of your thought. You may mentally center this thought form within yourself or in others as part of the visualization process. To a degree, sometimes great and sometimes small, the characteristics you've imparted to the thought form are transmitted into the energy being of another person or the energy constituents of a situation.

Either the person or situation may accept or reject the energy you've transmitted to them.

My consideration on these pages is not to teach the practice of mental healing, but to call attention to your influence upon life's higher energies and how, through the application of this process, you develop inner capacities and abilities suitable to life of a broader-than-normal scope.

Each day, when I finish writing on my computer, I tell it to "save" what I have written and add it to the file with which I am working. It automatically asks me if I wish the latest material to replace the previous information already in the file. If my answer is "yes" I then press the key marked "Enter" and the material is saved in the file.

This process is almost precisely duplicated in the automatic interaction between you and your file in the Records, with the exception that it's a continuous, ongoing procedure, non-stop, every day of your life. The everyday expression of your life energies is constantly deleting old and inputting new information in your Akashic Records file.

The true spiritual explorer will want to know more about the process, and will ask, "To improve my place in the Records, must I become a hermit or recluse, living a life of constant meditation and prayer?" Such a life may be perfect for a very few. For most it would not only be impossible, it would be unproductive.

It isn't reasonable to equate the rationale for birth on earth as being only for meditative purposes, or for the purpose of merely accepting a single avatar by name. Surely more is expected of us; we are in and on earth to "work" with spiritual energies in a material application. To grow by doing, to become more than we are, continuously. Your body is an energy center where the material and spiritual are combined, presenting the opportunity for self expression in combination with Divine expression.

And There WAS Light...

One of the ways in which you are in the image of God is that you are a creator. In the nature of that image, what better way to emulate the Divine than actually to use one of the highest of Divine creative energies—the Light. After the chaotic energies of lower and higher matter (earthly and heavenly electromagnetic particles) were organized into earth and the heavens (or higher planes), God said, "Let there be Light." So the opportunity we have on earth is to use that remarkable "substance" in our everyday lives—and to do so in a conscious and creative manner.

Light is not only an energy. It's endowed with the power of historic, cosmic symbolism. It represents openness, safety, the potency of good, inspiration, the realization of spirituality. Nothing grows without it. It heals. It encourages. It "lights the way." It makes the combination of body and spirit possible. It's a connector between the human being and the Akashic Records which, themselves, are but a higher range of light. And because of these all-important facets of light, it seems almost essential that the human being should learn to use, direct and control light consciously as one of the most pertinent and notable functions of life on earth.

As implausible as they may sound, I hope you will consider two possibilities—potentials inherent in your relationship with light. The first is that, although light seems nothing more than a pure energy form, it actually possesses characteristics other than mere luminescence, temperature, color and so on. It can serve as a carrier of the human voice as it does for your telephone conversations, for example. It can be tinged with feelings of indifference or caring. It can heal on many levels.

The second possibility is that in a subtle and elusive manner—just as subatomic particles are influenced by the mind of the nuclear research scientist—your relationship with light results in a slight modification of its qualities. As you use light, even the light from your floor lamp, you modify its atomic content with characteristics of your own being. This may occur either spontaneously or deliberately.

My family has told me that as an infant I was afflicted with a severe case of pneumonia during an epidemic of that disease. My grandfather's presence at my crib always resulted in a decrease in my fever—which did not occur in the presence of any other person.

My opinion on this? I accept the probability that the particular "light" of his being modified the natural light surrounding and within me toward that result. I agree that any such modification would be slight indeed, and that the natural light would retain intact most of its original nature. However I do not feel that a noticeable change in the characteristics of the light is necessary for a specific result to occur.

There will be more about this topic later in these pages. For the moment, the point is simply that we modulate higher vibrational ranges of light, non-consciously, as they connect us with the Akashic Records while we place upon them the resonant imprint of our thoughts and actions.

You set policy and edit by making choices. You make those choices by your value selections. They become the policy existing in your life. As they are reinforced by repetition, and prevail predominantly in your life expression, they assume a vibrational intensity which is recorded on the substance of the Book of Remembrance.

There may be periods during your life when you gradually, or perhaps suddenly, make changes in your value selections. If you maintain your changed policy, it in time deletes (or edits out) and replaces previous registrations in the Records, reflecting your new name or changed being.

Activities into which you are able to mentally direct energy contribute to value selections and policy changes. For example, let us imagine that you are faced with a necessary but unpleasant task. Before beginning the task itself, engage in some quiet time.

Remember, you're not trying to force your will on others, or insist upon your desire for the specific outcome of a situation. You are simply filling the vibrational nature of a person or situation with light. Mentally endow that light with the qualities of harmony, good for all persons concerned, strength, growth or any other important features you deem essential. Engaging in an activity of this nature is working with the light.

The inference that we may deduce from the above ideas is that we approach nearer the fulfillment of our missions on earth when we "work" with the light on a conscious as well as a non-conscious basis. The body you've selected is an energy center on the material plane, but it's also connected with higher planes. In the conduct of your life, you may feel that you only need to use physical plane energies. Or, if you are "on the path" you will wish consciously to incorporate higher energies with the lower, spiritual energies with the material, a combination of the two levels. You raise the lower by deliberately introducing the higher into its activities.

For an example let us assume that you are called upon to perform a very mundane task in which there seems to be no spirituality or other redeeming feature. Just before you begin, spend a few moments mentally "endowing" the energies involved in the work with your own sense of spirituality. Visualize those energies flowing through you and into the task and all the people associated with it. This is raising the lower by saturating it with the higher.

Remember, as editor you set the policy and supervise.

7

THE HIGHER EDIT...*Consciously managing light with your mind enables you to get through to the higher vibrational levels and the Akashic Records.*

Is it science fiction?

Science fiction is merely reality that has not yet appeared in objective form. Sooner or later it will do so. There is nothing hid that shall not be known.

Depending upon the nature of your belief system, you may at this point believe we're dealing with fiction. Or you may agree that our subject is spiritual science, a branch of the scientific disciplines which the various conventional Academies of Science aren't well equipped to study. I see it not as fiction but as a higher reality—a reality that is not yet universally perceived.

Hopefully, there will in the future be scientific studies revealing the relationship between the human individual and the phenomena of light. There already are studies about how light affects the individual. There should be research into the way the individual affects light.

Nearly half a century ago Dr. Pitirim Sorokin, at Harvard University, conducted experiments revealing the power of

love as an energy, exchangeable with other persons—and the
power of altruism, as it increased human longevity. (See his
book *The Ways and Power of Love*.) Perhaps the conveyor of
this energy was light. Through the years, I've drawn some
inferences from Dr. Sorokin's experiments and philosophy.
Principally, from my observations and intuitions, I believe
that the more you consciously interact with light through
expressions of mind and emotion, and the more your actions
are in accord with the positive vibrational elements of light,
the greater your significant "registrations" on the Akashic
Records.

Science in the future—will it continue to research the
human affinity for the light: physically, emotionally,
mentally and spiritually? And will it ultimately see what the
mystic sees, and know what the mystic knows? Will science
research the ways in which you can mentally manage the
energies of light for healing, for expressing care, and
comfort, protection and strength? Until this occurs, it's
important for you and me, and others of like mind, to engage
in our "anecdotal" research so that one day the hallowed
halls of academia will open doorways to "higher" scientific
research. Then the speculative will become the empirical. In
the meantime, let us do a little spiritual theorizing, based on
anecdotal and intuitive experience.

Our word *mystic* is from ancient obscure (probably
Greek) sources meaning, literally, "with closed eyes."
However, it isn't to be taken as indicating that a mystic
should become blinded to physical sight or reality. It
signifies that to temporarily close out or ignore the physical
sense of sight is apt to activate a higher, inner sense of
sight. The physical sense interferes with, or overpowers, the
spiritual—until the individual sets a different policy. The
policy needs to include, at least for many of us, spiritual

inferences which we may draw from personal experiences.

We may be in the infancy of our understanding of light and our relationship to it. For example, how often do we hear the sound which light makes, or see the light which emanates from sound?

Many persons (including some symphony orchestra conductors) have had the experience of seeing colors while certain tonal combinations are sounded by a musical group. I don't know that it has been experimented with but I consider it possible that persons with a certain kind of sensitivity, even though blindfolded, might be able to detect different colors of light by the sounds of light energy which fall upon their inner ear. We may infer that the qualities of light permeate many levels of vibrational energies and, in doing so, engage in a harmonious interplay of vital life with them.

Life Flows 24 Hours a Day

In our outer, everyday life we attempt to maintain an organized continuity—daylight to night, to daylight once more, over and over again. A rhythm is established which enables us to conduct our affairs, play, get our rest, return to a scheduled day, on and on, based on cyclical sunlight. But with our "eyes closed," an analogy for mystically limiting a lower form of light the better to "see" with a higher, we note that the light of the Akashic Records also serves to maintain a much more organized continuity of life for each of us. It isn't the repetitive, bustling continuity of cyclical time and space. Ignoring those two qualities completely, the Records hold communion with cycles of soul energy and the primary substance from which the latter emerged.

If it could be tested, it's my belief you would discover that the *quantity* of your thinking with the nighttime levels of your consciousness might be less than with your normal daytime levels. However, the *quality* of nighttime thinking would be higher and more satisfying. My reasoning is that daytime thinking is scattered, scampering off in all directions, due to literally hundreds of distractions. It is less easily controlled or organized. Nighttime thinking, on the other hand, is freed from the attachments and disturbances of your body and its needs, your surroundings, family, vocation and a thousand other often distressing and limiting details. Nighttime thinking, through channels of higher mind and spirit, is better attuned to upper dimensions. It is thus in a position for better interaction with the Akashic Records.

In seminars around the world for many years, I've taught an idea which I refer to as the *Continuum of Consciousness*. A variation of the process is known to psychologists as *The Evening Review*. To describe the idea briefly, we begin with the fact that during the day you encounter experiences which are sometimes very meaningful to you. To the best of your ability, you save these experiences in your memory in order to create what you hope is a connected, satisfying life. At night, though your normal consciousness is subdued, your higher consciousness is active, and is having *its* experiences independently of your body, and in a higher dimension or higher plane of reality. To gain the greatest benefit from experiences on both planes of reality, there should be a continuum or connectedness between the events of the day and the night. Often there is none.

Why is such a relationship necessary? To deliberately and consciously· connect the seemingly separate events of day and night, happenings on two planes of life expression, into one seamless flow. As the editor of your life journal, you should set policy and supervise the smooth transition from daytime to nighttime experiences so that all the more or less independent levels of your consciousness will function harmoniously.

The goal is to relate major life events to each other to obtain from them the greatest possible mental and spiritual evolvement. If such a relationship is left to chance, or lack of direction, evolvement occurs haphazardly. Becoming involved with the process on a conscious level contributes to organization and coordination of both normal and higher levels of consciousness. In other words, a productive continuum is created. Through it, the meanings of significant daytime and nighttime events often become centered in your normal conscious level, life takes on new meaning, and an inner satisfaction concerning life is often enhanced.

Here is the process for engaging in *Consciousness Continuum* (the Evening Review). Before retiring, mentally, rapidly, review whatever you consider the day's meaningful events, if any. While reviewing each scene in your mind's eye, let it be filled with an aura of white light. If the day has contained more than one such special event, begin with the last special occurrence of the day, think it through quickly *as an observer, not a participant*, as though you were watching a movie. Then go backward to the next to the last event, review it in the same way, and so on through the day toward the beginning. Do this as though you were watching a movie being displayed in an aura of light.

Remember, begin with the last event and move progressively toward the first. Remember, too, to be an observer, not a participant in the scenes you recall. If you allow yourself to participate in the scene, you become involved in emotional levels which are a distraction. You are not judging, changing or in any other way influencing your recollection. The reason for progressing backwards through the day's events is that doing so usually enhances the clarity of remembrance. If your mind wanders from the scene you are recalling, begin again. If you fall asleep, do not let that fact be disappointing to you the next day.

What you have reviewed in this fashion often gives direction to your experiences during sleep while your body is at rest but your higher consciousness is active. Your higher mind "connects" with important details of the day and carries on in the same or a similar mode. Thus the continuum of the night experience is related to the day experience, and begins adding to it. The result may be explanatory "dreams" of which you become aware—or often there will be astral and higher experiences which surface and unfold in your consciousness at a later time. Thus the affairs of the day following your practice of a Consciousness Continuum session become a continuum of the previous night's experiences.

In this practice, then, an organized "flow" of your life begins to unfold. You are "playing out" both dharma and karma more easily and rapidly. Day and night are both enhanced by the light you've mentally directed to the process. They complement each other, and contribute to each other. And they've done so through the connection you established with the Akashic Records by including "the light" in the process.

The more you deliberately and consciously interact with the light, particularly in its higher vibratory ranges, the better your connection with the Akashic Records. It isn't necessary that you constantly remind yourself of this fact. When your inner association with the range of spiritual energies which is symbolized by the light becomes to some degree habitual, your interaction with the Records becomes natural and regular rather than haphazard. The organized interplay of unstated information flows better in both directions, both to and from the Records. You maintain an organized continuity through the years of your physical lifetime. And further, organized continuity is maintained through a series of incarnations.

Many good things happen when the power of light is used. I'm told that many years ago, in England, a group of children afflicted with jaundice were confined in a ward in which windows were located along one side of the room only. A nurse noted that children closest to the windows recovered more rapidly than those whose beds were further away. As a result, light became one of the treatments for jaundice. Perhaps elements of the children's bodies were stimulated by the sunlight, and in turn they communicated the energy in its healing form throughout the body so that recovery of health became possible.

Remove Undesirable Records

It is known that various parts of your body communicate with each other through electronic impulses, which are a form of light. And just as the Akashic Records are, in effect, extensions of your life, you may wonder if there is a way to "heal," or change, any portion of the Records which contain information you'd rather not have there. Are you concerned that some intentional wrongdoing on your part has left its imprint on your higher record? Or that an unintentional folly will mar it? This was a concern to the ancients just as it is for us today.

If a Biblical analogy is of interest to you, possibly the *Book of Isaiah* has an answer. As the prophet told his followers while speaking on behalf of the Infinite, "I AM he who blots out your transgressions...and will not remember your sins any more."

The significance of this statement could be that turning

to Spirit in your life removes the vibrational imprint of your lesser qualities from your page in the Book of God's Remembrance. To change your file, turn to the dimensions of Spirit. Become one with the Light.

You may wonder what I mean by saying, "...turn to the dimensions of Spirit." Certainly I'm not suggesting that you must become a saint. Nor will I propose that correcting a mistake, unintentional or deliberate, is as simple as merely erasing the Records mentally and replacing them. If you feel there is something of your life registered on the Records which you would rather not have there, some serious introspection is called for. Remember, the Records do not judge you—they are part of the process of your judging yourself. *They do not judge the deed—they record and reflect the nature of the motive.* You must ask yourself what element of your own being has contributed to the unwanted record— and strive to eliminate it. So, how is that accomplished?

Changing your page in the Book of God's Remembrance, the Akashic Records, is no Easy-Take-Out, fast food drive through type of procedure. All the characteristics of cosmic energies come to focus on your page. They are not dealt with lightly. They inexorably reflect every nuance of every aspect of your being. Broadly speaking, earth is in the lower plane of work; primary substance is the higher plane of maintaining a record of that work. Think of it as for your benefit rather than your judgment; your dharma as well as your karma; your opportunity rather than your obstacle.

Without many of its nuances, your life mission may be divided into two extensive categories: outer goals, consisting of objectives that are exterior to your immediate person, and inner goals, relating to your self and its evolvement toward supreme realization of your spiritual potentials.

In your mind, imagine the inner qualities you believe to

be "of the Spirit." If you are in the Divine image, what lights of that image have been fragmented and deposited in your being? If you are a spark of the Divine flame, in what way are the qualities of that flame glimmering in you?

What weakness needs to be strengthened? What strength needs to be reinforced? What lack needs to be filled? What negative needs to be eliminated and replaced?

God is a fire (a light) that does not consume. God is righteousness that does not judge. God is strength that does not coerce. God is joy that takes no advantage of others. God is love that expects no return.

Decide which qualities of your self (qualities, not outer goals) you wish to center upon as being part of your life's mission, to improve during your incarnation. Take time to think this through calmly and thoroughly. Then, decide exactly what steps you will take to achieve the spiritual evolvement you seek in your life. The steps you take, and maintain, automatically delete the negative fields in your Record and replace them with positives.

Any wrong you might have committed unintentionally is easily repaired. The wrong that is done intentionally is more difficult to rectify for it reflects a predominating mental ambience or pattern. To erase it from your page in "the book" requires changing the pattern, which replaces the unwanted motif, and maintaining that change. This eventually establishes the new information on the Record. You set the policy, which is *the change of pattern*—and you supervise its continuation, which is *maintaining the change*. As you think in your mind is one matter; as you think in your heart is another. And it is the latter that makes the more indelible impression upon the Records.

There are three expressions of the human spirit which might well be considered analogous to the Divine Spirit, and thus closely affiliated with the primary substance of the Akashic Records. They are *altruism*, *love* and *light*.

There's a vibrational relationship between these three that may someday be explored scientifically for the benefit of humankind. Until then, you must explore for yourself, and thus help create an atmosphere of receptivity for such an idea when its time is ripe for planting in the scientific consciousness.

Altruism, a "concern for the welfare of others," is an extension of the concept that all life is one. It is giving back to life those seeds of the "fruit" which life has made available to you. It's the practical though unselfish expression of life energy. A tree or plant returns the seeds of its life to the earth from whence it came. A human being should return the "seeds" of his or her life to the plane of spirit from whence it came.

The dictionary defines love as an "affection." In my opinion that's a pretty paltry description of an energy as powerful as love. I think love is a human extension of a Divine quality. It's a powerful energy potential, vibrationally similar to the Divine expression toward all life—though you and I may frequently focus it rather narrowly. And there's not necessarily anything wrong with our doing that.

The quality of your altruism and love is indicated by the purity of motive with which they are expressed. And the purity of motive determines the nature of their imprint upon the Records.

Love is spontaneous; altruism is intentional. Both imply the proper management of your life, its values, and its energies. All the energies of life with which you become associated take on the distinctive quality of your personal characteristics.

The physical scientist will tell you there is no human emotion in pure energy. I'm not certain of this. God is love. The vibrations of love are hidden deeply in the subatomic particles of primary substance. Love is an energy. Love is a special type of energy which is infused with a distinctive quality. In your case it is the uncommon quality of your unique life. Love to the best of your potential for love.

Light. In a philosophical sense it's an appropriate symbol. In the realm of spiritual science it's a powerful energy. The scriptures of all religions use its many connotations to instruct, inspire, strengthen.

"God is light," says the *First Epistle of John.*

"You are the light of the world," said Jesus in the *Gospel of Matthew.*

"God is the light of heaven and earth," said Muhammed in the *Koran.*

"Ahura Mazda is the Lord (source) of Light," contended Zoroaster.

Each of these statements is significant in its own way, but let's take just a moment to consider the implications of Zoroaster's. Ahura Mazda is known as the God of Light. The word Ahura means spirit. Mazda means wise. So Ahura Mazda may come nearer a description of God than any other name we have—Wise Spirit—pure spirit, or light, with the attribute of wisdom embodied in it. An alternate Zoroastrian name for God is Ormazd, which means the "source of Light."

In your own meditations you may find yourself comfortable thinking of the Divine Being as the presence of Light, pure spirit, endowed with wisdom—and present around and in you. This, of course, is merely a suggestion for those who find it difficult to personify God into a super human being.

Light. This first emanation from primary substance, shares its origination with all humanity. In this Aquarian Age, it does seem important that we return to the roots of our being, rediscover our kinship with light, familiarize ourselves with its potencies and learn to use them.

8

GETTING IN TOUCH...*the computer mechanism is merely an extension of the human
being; what the human creates the computer
simulates.*

Is it possible to get in touch with your future through the
Akashic Records? No, because the future isn't there except
in potential. Only the past is registered on its pages.

However, the nature of your future, and the trend of your
future, may be deciphered, or "read," from your personal
page. Your future is tentatively on your Record in the form
of the past and its vibrational imprint. And the past, when
observed and analyzed, merely indicates the trend the future
is taking if not changed. Thus the future is offered only on a
provisional basis.

A consideration of the future as a group of specific and
unchangeable details indicates an uncompromising fate over
which you have no control. That isn't the nature of the
universe. *Any* change in the present changes the future.
Every change in the present changes the future. Perhaps not
always as fully as you would like, but always to some
degree. So getting in touch with your Record provides you

with information about the past and present which then empowers you for changing the future.

With this thought in mind, it is easier to see that getting in touch with the Records becomes a method of personal evolvement, just as history is used (or should be) by humankind en masse. Humankind evolves from the lessons of history. The record is in history books. You evolve through the lessons of personal experience. Your record is in the Book of God's Remembrance, the Akashic Records.

But how do you read the book?

Let's begin with memory. One needs only to observe a court trial to learn that memories of a specific detail are often faulty. And that they often change. And frequently fail. Probably you've also noticed that when an important detail drops from your memory, the more pressure you exert attempting to recall it the more difficult it is to remember. The reason for this is that to remember from the cluttered surface of your mind is often close to impossible. So instead of continuing that unsuccessful attempt, on special occasions it may be less difficult to go to the Akashic Records for help.

Meditation is the time honored way. Do not trust drugs for they produce synthetic experiences—which are real, but not valid in the spiritual sense. Aids, such as music and incense, are helpful for some, not for others. Spontaneous or controlled flashbacks and regressions of this and previous lives often lead to Akashic Record contacts.

One of today's popular methods for contacting the Records, especially in the context of past incarnations, is through hypnosis. The process isn't limited to uncovering hidden or suppressed memories, though it is excellent for that purpose. Under the direction of an expert practitioner, hypnosis may free the consciousness to awareness on higher vibratory levels—on some occasions the levels of primary substance and the vibratory information which has been recorded there.

"Reading" the Records is a term that may include a number of psychic activities—clairvoyance, or seeing visions; clairaudience, or hearing inner but outwardly silent sounds; psychometry, or detecting inner sensations of a feeling nature. In these quite different but related perceptive functions, an inner transducer is somehow automatically activated. Our relationship with light comes alive. This is one of the remarkable features of a human being. He or she is capable of receiving (or inputting) energy in one form, then converting (or outputting) it in another form. Thus, for example, an energy form that is inwardly felt becomes "transduced" into an energy form that is perceived as a vision, a seemingly audible sound, or an inwardly sentient feeling.

Here's one way of making a safari into the realms of spiritual life. You may wish to experiment with this meditational journey as a way to get in touch with the Records, to "read" them as a helpful chronicle of your life, the causes of its problems and the course of its potentials. It's a method of visiting Akasha—Cosmic Sky—and the special environs of primary substance you've conditioned and configured with your own vibrational inscription.

After reading the following, before actually engaging in the meditation, you may wish to record on audio tape the material printed in italics. Being guided by your own voice in the meditation may help make it more effective. You may also wish to create your own narration.

Assume any meditation pose in which you can be relaxed as fully as possible. Any yogic posture that does not create muscular strain, a straight or easy chair, or even lying down, all positions are acceptable. Then speak your version of the following, or listen to your own voice on tape. There should be pauses between sentences as you "read," by means of your inner faculties—receptivity and sensitivity to your vibrational field in the Record. What do you inwardly "see," "hear," "feel," as you entertain the following meditative thoughts?

> *I seek the realm of Akasha, Cosmic Sky, wherein abides the Primary Substance of the universe—*
> *I seek it not as an object at a distance in space, but as it resides and manifests within the vibrational complex of my entire being—*
> *I seek Akasha for the purpose of evolvement—that I might grow in understanding, in knowledge, in spirituality, in creativity, in wisdom—*
> *I withdraw more deeply from the material attractions and vibrational demands upon my awareness—*
> *Now I find myself floating free from those entanglements, and ready to explore the higher life. I am saturated throughout my being with the good of that life as well as its freedom—*
> *I do not attempt to change others. I mean to change myself only, and only for the good—*
> *I am free, with my awareness becoming more and more centered in Akasha. I seek for, and ask for, guidance upon my path—*
> *What do I need to change in myself?—*
> *What special qualities have I acquired in the past that will help me change myself? And thus improve the future?*

Be still...as you await any inner perceptions that may come to you. After what you perceive to be a reasonable length of this quiet time, express your appreciation—give thanks—for your contact with the Records and for help given you by higher dimensional energies and persons. Give yourself a few moments to return to your normal level of consciousness and your relationship with your surroundings. You are then ready for the next step in the procedure.

The above completes the attunement process. Now continue with the next step, which is to analyze the impressions, intuitive insights or other inner "receptions" you may have experienced.

Perhaps you do not immediately become aware of any response. Remember you are attempting a feat, or rather a discipline, that is not easily or quickly accomplished. For most persons, practice, patience and perseverance will be required. There is no legitimate shortcut.

After giving yourself time to analyze any responses you become aware of, make notes of your sensations and your interpretation of them. Keep the notes for occasional review, for sometimes they are later capable of revealing additional interpretation and further clarification. They may reveal more self changes which foster your self evolvement and an improvement of the conditions of your life. Remember, you're not engaging in self fortune telling. You're seriously determining the trend of your life as it is, and what should be done to alter that trend, if advisable.

You're considering the only two possible aspects of change in your life: what you *do* and what you *think*. So to help you objectify your observations, you may want to gauge them against the following criteria:

In what way should I change what I am doing? What should I do that I am not doing? What should I not do that I am doing?

And: In what way should I change what I am thinking? What should I think that I am not thinking? What should I not think that I am thinking?

There are additional methods and inner self exercises which will increase your sensitivity and the success of your getting in touch with your Record.

One of the ways to improve your ability to contact the Akashic Records is to experiment with *Psychometry*, a word which means to "measure the soul." It's a psychic function, usually connected with the sense of inner feeling through outer physical contact with an object. Holding a small article in one's hands, or touching it if it is large, leads to sensing the nature of the energies embedded within it. The "vibrations" felt, or inwardly sensed in this manner are interpreted as offering details of the life of the object and its owner or principal user. The faculty used in psychometry is often termed *clairsentience*, literally meaning "clear feeling."

Contact with the Akashic Records results in a similar clairsentient feeling experience and it fulfills the literal meaning of the word psychometry or soul measuring. Experiments with psychometry, and practicing them with friends or family, increase inner sensitivity. They also teach the valuable lesson that perfection in the practice is impossible, and that one should carefully analyze any such perceptions with the logical mind before relying on them too seriously.

The simple way to practice psychometry is to seek the aid of family or friends for help in experimenting. Ask them to give you an article they've carried on their person (a pen, key, gemstone, watch, etc.) or worn (a ring or other item of jewelry) over an extended period of time. Hold the article between your hands for a few moments of stillness as you direct your consciousness to be receptive to subtle feelings that seem to flow from the article and become centered within you. Describe the feelings to the article's owner for confirmation or denial of their correctness. Continued practice should result in improved accuracy.

There's a similarity between an experience with psychometry and a contact with the Akashic Records. Both are the inner sensing of vibrational energies in the form of feelings, followed by mental and intuitive interpretation of the meaning and significance of those feelings.

For some, the use of crystals and various gemstones are an aid to the psychometric process of attunement to the Records. They find a special crystal, for example, for which they have an affinity. It "feels good" when held in one's hand, or is in close view. Because crystals and a variety of gemstones sometimes help to stimulate inner psychic activities, they may make it easier to enter the inner and higher levels of consciousness, the higher self and beyond. And because some crystals, including diamonds, amplify higher vibrational energies some persons find them helpful in attempting to get in touch with the Records. Concentrating visually on the crystal, or holding it in your hands as you meditate for contact with the records, assists some persons in this attunement process.

A variation of the psychometric methods previously described is to attempt to "tune in" with other forms of life. An animal pet, a flower or shrub, a tree or its leaf, all possess their own unique variations of the One Great Life. It's my observation that a way to become more aligned with the One Life is to practice awareness of various aspects of that life. To do this, attempt to feel within yourself whatever that form of life may be feeling within itself. A few experiences of this nature increase appreciation of the One

Life, as well as expand and increase the possibility of attunement with the Records.

I further suggest, regarding your experiments with psychometry—a refinement which I refer to as "selective tuning." As you are meditating with an object held in your hand, mentally state, "I am becoming attuned to the *physical* level of the vibratory energies around and within this object." Then pause while inwardly sensing any responses that may enter your mind concerning the physical body of the object's owner. Next, mentally make the same statement regarding the *emotional* level of vibratory energies. After waiting a few moments for responses to be received, continue the procedure by directing your consciousness to consider the *mental* and finally the *spiritual* levels of the vibrational energies, in each instance waiting for inner responses, if any. Use your own mind to direct the attunement to the specifically selected vibrational levels. Doing so is a positive and organized step toward the realization of valid results. Otherwise one is creating an uncontrolled and unorganized receptivity to just *any* kind of result. Apply this same selective tuning method to your experiments for getting in touch with the Records on your own behalf.

Each of the attunement methods given here and in this and other sections of this book has its own limitations and advantages. Each will be more effective for some persons and less so for others. Your own experiments must determine which one, or combination, is best for you. The important detail is to learn to "read" inwardly with objectivity, which isn't easy. There should be no biased assumptions regarding the information you receive in the process. There should be no judgments, no emotional inferences, no leaping to conclusions concerning possibly important changes in your life, without very careful consideration of consequences. Never forget, *you* set the policy and supervise the activity. Consequently, the results are your responsibility.

Your interest in the preceding information, what it means to you, what it can do for you, is a legitimate concern. I cannot promise what it will do for you. I'm reluctant to tell you what it has accomplished in my own life. I'm hesitant to do so, for I would not want you to think I've reached any special spiritual state, which I haven't. But I do recognize that my life has changed as a result of my beliefs and experiences, the Akashic Records among them. Those changes are here noted merely as indicators of what you can accomplish, if you wish, and with all reverence for the one who first expressed the idea, I'm sure you can "do even more." Here, then, is the list for your consideration, your acceptance or rejection as you may be inclined.

My study of and experiences with the Akashic Records have for me produced *some* degree of each of the following: increased appreciation of life, both here and hereafter; expanded respect for others, in that we all truly share the One Life; increased regard for other forms of life; an improved sense of empathy; greater understanding of meaning and purpose in life; a degree of sensitivity and response to the Records and to other people; more understanding of the process of life's continuity and how it is maintained.

As I look back from time to time on my own experiences, I realize that inner affinities (often on a non-conscious level) have led me into extremely satisfying situations and philosophical concepts. This is particularly true of the way we all share in the One Life. To learn whether or not this is also true in your life, let's spend a few moments looking at *affinities*.

9

AFFINITIES...*Are the Records of value to individuals only, or do they serve a usefulness common to all?*

Symbiosis is the relationship between two or more different organisms in a close association that may or may not be of benefit to each of them. Symbiosis, in the context of this book, results from the expression of affinities between you and another person, or you and a specific type of thought—or you and the Akashic Records.

For our purpose, symbiosis refers to energies of similar or harmonious vibrational wavelengths. An affinity is symbiosis in action. That's an involved way of stating the old folk saying that, "Birds of a feather flock together." Or the metaphysical precept that, "Like attracts like."

Affinities—and the Records—are they useful only to individuals, or do they, in their symbiotic relationships, benefit everyone? To answer, we must look into both possibilities.

Ordinarily we think of affinities as personal attractions for one another, as individuals. But, to spiritual science, the word also means the vast shared attraction of all forms of life, which indicates that we share a common origin. That origin isn't physical. Your body didn't create your mind, or your spirit—your spirit and your mind helped create your body. Before incarnation your mind and spirit found (I'm going to create a word here)—found an *affiniation* of physical plane energies and circumstances. For your own purposes you chose to participate in molding and inhabiting that affiniation (which was a body in the process of formation in a specific environment) temporarily. In doing so, you fulfilled another meaning of the word affinity—which is that certain atomic structures unite with other atomic structures and remain in the merged state.

Just as persons have and constantly create affinities through the exercise of their life patterns, so also do aggregate modes of thought, such as science and religion. The fact that science has one set of affinities and religion has another, is not in itself a bad situation. It is when adherents of those affinities are determined to make them exclusive of each other, and superior over each other, that a disservice is done to all humankind.

Conventional science gives us an airplane, but no pilot.

Conventional religion gives us a pilot, but no airplane.

Therefore, both science and religion serve us partially; neither serves us properly. But to be honest, the dividing line between them is neither harsh nor rigid. Persons on both sides of the street dividing science and religion are still neighbors. In the terms of this book, both have unrealized affinities for the other.

So in reference to the Akashic Records, it seems to me we should be both scientist and religionist. We must have the plane *and* the pilot. Emerson has said that, "We are adapted to infinity." Therefore do we not have an affinity for the wisdom and substance of infinite life, part of that substance being the Akashic Records? We are inherently drawn to the eternal. We gravitate toward it. We yearn for it. In our often misguided and cumbersome way we strive for it.

The scientist who doesn't believe in the eternal life of the human spirit, nevertheless strives his utmost to prolong life. In my opinion this is a reflection, however slight, of his inner affinity with never ending life. The religionist who decries modern science doesn't realize that its many forms and discoveries are approaching the realms and energies of life's spiritual dimensions. In the ever-strange way of life, seeming opposites such as science and religion, have affinities for each other. In the boundless scheme of things beyond our understanding, they are slowly converging on the same path.

In a similar fashion, you and I, though seeming to be distantly separated from the Akashic Records, are probably approaching a greater awareness of their existence and their purpose in our infinite lives. We're learning that the letter of the law is the law of the physical plane, while the spirit of the law is the law of the spiritual plane. The planes exist and interpenetrate each other with their own form of—my new word again—affiniation.

Live in the Ambience of the Higher Life

So there is a kind of cosmic affinity, holding us and our world and our universe together in compliance with a combination of physical and spiritual law that is beyond our comprehension.

Many persons more or less isolate themselves from any affinity with the Greater Life. This doesn't mean they are reclusive, selfish, egotistical or afraid. It means simply that they do not sufficiently use their capacity to let life energies flow *in* to themselves—and *out* to others. They just don't always participate in what I think of as *life ambience.*

Ordinarily, ambience relates to the nature of surroundings

and is considered only in a mundane sense, the ambience or pleasant surroundings of a restaurant, or an office building, for example. To me, life ambience is the nature and amount of energy flow in and out of your life and its relationship to other energies and planes, including the Akashic Records. It is still, of course, the nature of your surroundings. But you are always an integral part of your surroundings, and they are part of you.

Your surroundings, however, aren't limited to the physical world, which is itself permeated with invisible energies. Nor is it limited to the horizontal world of physical space. There is also a vertical relationship between you and your surroundings—vertical in the sense of higher than physical dimension planes, such as those on which the Akashic Records are found.

When we mentally and emotionally set our life patterns we create life ambience. We condition the often unrealized inward and outward flow of life energies, resulting in both vertical and perpendicular ambience. There's a constant networking of energies in life that unifies them and gives us the opportunity to use them all for self growth. The power of affinities to enhance one another individually, and en masse, is unlimited. Or, we should say, it is limited only by our ability to work with them on a conscious basis.

What is the life ambience I've created? Does it limit me to horizontal affinities which cause me to live by the "jump from the frying pan into the fire" syndrome? Or does it free me to experience vertical experiences also? Expand the extent of my vision? Enable me to gain the greatest possible amount of *both* physical plane and spiritual plane growth? How does it all fit together? The final section of this work offers you a simplified and organized view of the living affinities in your life, and their relationship to the Akashic Records.

10

LET'S LOOK AT THE WHOLE PICTURE...
*the cosmic view of the Akashic Records, their
meaning in your life, and how you get in touch
with them.*

In the *Tao Teh Ching*, Lao Tze speaks cryptically of
"going back to one's roots." He suggests that in doing so
your destiny and its relationship to eternal law is
discovered. Returning to your historical roots is helpful, but
your real roots are in primary substance, for the unique roots
of your individual life are in the Akashic Records. Lao Tze
also says that to know the eternal law is to achieve
enlightenment.

Your reading thus far indicates that you possess a broad
range of sensitive consciousness capable of considering
cosmic possibilities which most persons would reject out of
hand. So I have a question for you:

> Are the Akashic Records, and the primary
> substance on which they are registered,
> humanity's link with eternity?

Do you and I, conscious of our seeming mortality,

nevertheless maintain a connection with our immortality through the Records? Are they the real roots from which we sprouted into earth life, and to which we return at physical death? Are they the basic substance of God through which we are fabricated and formed in His likeness?

For a holistic view of one cycle of life, may I paraphrase for you just a few verses of the 139th Psalm as translated into English from the Aramaic by Dr. George Lamsa. This is a personal rephrasing of the Psalm for the purpose of applying it to your life today.

Imagine it is close to midnight and you are a lonely shepherd, seated on a hillside while your flock sleeps. The sky is star filled. The night is totally silent. Thoughts of life's wonders and eternity, and your connection with them, drift through your consciousness.

"Even the darkness has its light for me," you muse to yourself. Then you slowly continue your reflections.

"The night is as the day, for both darkness and light are filled with thy spirit—

"Out of your pure substance you created me and accompanied me on my journey to earth through the body of my mother. It is a marvel that heaven and earth can be thus united—

"You have seen me in this lower substance, a combination of the perfect and the imperfect—and it all was written in your books before day was and humankind was brought into existence—

"Lead me in the everlasting way—"

Your serenity and the night's blend in an ecstacy of an abiding, undisturbed, long continuing oneness.

We "live"—and "die"—and live again. The cycles are more than a continuum of consciousness. They're a continuum of life. Your connection with the Records provides you with:

* a review of your plan for incarnation and a strategy for carrying out that plan;
* a map of the highroads and byroads you've followed, and a description of your experiences along the way;
* a record of your errors, to be sure, but more importantly a record of your improvements and accomplishments.

In short, the Records enable you to be the editor—to set policy and supervise. To use the eternal light consciously. Let's look at more details.

The Gnostics believed that being a Christian required more than faith alone. They believed that one must transcend faith and learn to use the energies which Jesus used. Among them, the higher energy which could be likened only to light.

The Gospel According to Thomas is part of a collection of *The Sayings of Jesus* contained in an ancient Coptic text. The text was discovered in a tomb close to what was once an active Gnostic community near Nag Hamadi, Egypt. In Thomas's Gospel, it is stated that, in a conversation with his disciples, Jesus gave the following instructions:

If people ask you where you originated, tell them that, "We have come from the Light, where the Light originated through itself."

And in continuing this conversation he said that when others ask you what is a sign of the Father's presence within you, tell them that, "It is a movement and a rest."

Among some of the ancients, creation is known as the emergence of the "hidden light" from the Divine Being. We are beings of light. We've specialized our existence, forged out of primary substance, as individual lights. We are the light that goeth not out. The embers of eternity are always aglow within us, awaiting those special occasions that fan them aflame with the fire that does not burn.

Our bodies are phased in and out of expression time and again—the cycles of movement and rest are ever active in us, just as they are throughout the universe. On spirals of incarnational and post-incarnational levels, the self which is in a state of comparative darkness suddenly becomes translucent with light. A new concept, basically a new understanding, is added to one's being. That self then seeks a higher level among the ever-broadening spirals upon which to repeat the process. When this happens to you, you will recognize it by the fact that the full realization of a new reality illumines your consciousness.

"The one who knows himself has insight," said Lao Tze.

"To the one who has (understanding), even more is given," said Jesus.

Potential. The inherent ability or capacity for growth, development, or coming into being. You have the potential for acquiring greater knowledge about yourself, and greater understanding.

To "know yourself" implies knowing more than what you've done, or become. If it is to give you true insight, knowing yourself must cast a light on what greater things you are capable of doing, being, or understanding. Present performance is important; future performance is more so, for it provides the opportunity for your potentials to be expressed. Each member of the human race has greater potential than anyone realizes. Let the following words—I think they're Tennyson's—inspire you to reach out for the potential which the Akashic Records may help you discover.

> *Within me is the sum of all things past.*
> *Within me are the years that yet remain,*
> *And heaven has not a space too high nor vast,*
> *That I may not within myself contain,*
> *Nor is there an accomplishment divine*
> *That is not slumbering in this soul of mine.*

Attunement to the Records adds a new dimension to life. Life on the physical level we know quite well. Life in conjunction with the spiritual level is one with which we have a measure of familiarity. Life on the higher spiritual level of primary substance, through conscious interaction with the Akashic Records, is somewhat like connecting with a new neighbor. We've met, but we haven't yet come to know each other very well. But we do possess the potential for growth and understanding, the potential for discovering and awakening the slumbering "accomplishment Divine" that is within us.

In this age, when religion and science are each trying to lay claim to the other's turf while protecting their own, humankind needs to find eternal roots. Vision beyond any commonly known present limitations is vital. There are those of us who have the vision to recognize that we are all of one substance, even though we have particularized ourselves into various "names." To emphasize the differences between us, and disregard the parallels, is an error of cosmic immensity—whether it is on an individual or a global scale.

The claims of supremacy and sovereignty by both religion and science are totally out of proper character for each. Truly a tragedy. Possibly in some future day, when we find our roots in the primary substance we all share in common, we will have world peace. Perhaps even galactic peace! We *must* have it, and we *can* have it, because, after all, the idea of a soul mate connection isn't a concept limited to two people only, for...

WE ARE ALL SOUL MATES!

Index

The publisher of this book is a nonprofit
organization presenting metaphysical,
mystical, philosophical and self-help
material. For more information write:

Astara Administration Building
792 W. Arrow Hwy.
Upland, CA 91786